T0161281

THE AMERICAN POETRY REVIEW/HONICKMAN
FIRST BOOK PRIZE

The Honickman Foundation is dedicated to the support of projects that promote spiritual growth and creativity, education and social change. At the heart of the mission of the Honickman Foundation is the belief that creativity enriches contemporary society because the arts are powerful tools for enlightenment, equity and empowerment, and must be encouraged to effect social change as well as personal growth. A current focus is on the particular power of photography and poetry to reflect and interpret reality, and, hence, to illuminate all that is true.

The annual American Poetry Review/Honickman First Book Prize offers publication of a book of poems, a $3,000 award, and distribution by Copper Canyon Press through Consortium. Each year a distinguished poet is chosen to judge the prize and write an introduction to the winning book. The purpose of the prize is to encourage excellence in poetry, and to provide a wide readership for a deserving first book of poems. *Uttermost Paradise Place* is the twelfth book in the series.

UTTERMOST

PARADISE

PLACE

UTTERMOST
PARADISE
PLACE

Laura McKee

Winner of the APR/Honickman First Book Prize

The American Poetry Review
Philadelphia

Distribution by Copper Canyon Press/Consortium.

Library of Congress Control Number:

ISBN 978-0-9776395-8-8 (cloth, alk. paper)
ISBN 978-0-9776395-7-1 (pbk., alk. paper)

FIRST EDITION

Book design and composition by Valerie Brewster, Scribe Typography

For my parents

ACKNOWLEDGEMENTS

Poems in this manuscript have appeared in the following publications/
venues: "Red Fur Cello" (excerpt) in *Konundrum,* "Geometry and a
Letter" in *Identity Theory,* "Strategy for the Decline" in *Birds and Whistles,*
"A Finite Piece of Furniture-Sized Light" in *Mid-American Review,* "Paper
Cut" (excerpt) in *Rhino,* and "Letter to My Aunt" in *Campbell's Corner.*
"Wonder," "Horses and Monarchs," and "Weak Anthropic Principle"
were part of a gallery showing at Studio 128.

Also, this manuscript was written during time afforded by generous grants
from the Seattle Arts Commission and the Jackstraw Writers Program.

Contents

What a Bad Idea to Come Out This Far   3

Glacier 1   4

The Solution   5

Sun On One   6

Geometry and a Letter   7

Billboard 1   8

Pregnant Headless Clown   9

Wet Feet   10

Many Beautiful Stories   11

Ekphrastic Dream 1   12

Death of a Blue Vase   13

The Last Wall is a Strange Cool Puzzle   15

Strategy for the Decline   16

Notes from Mr. Aday   17

A Finite Piece of Furniture-Sized Light   18

Swan Brothers 1   19

Unweighted Nymphs in Still Waters   20

The Tally   21

Glacier 2   22

Letter to My Aunt   23

Smaller   24

Anderson   25

Paper Cut   26

Glacier 3   29

Unlike Paradise   30

Women, Weight, and Weightlessness   31

Billboard 2   32

Horses and Monarchs   33

Do Not Confuse Opportunity with Certainty   34

Swan's Trail Road   35

Billboard 3   36

Care and Feeding of the Faux Fur Coat   37

Afterlife   38

Glacier 4   39

Neighborhoods at Dusk   40

Ekphrastic Dream 2   41

Lockets   42

Weak Anthropic Principle   43

Ekphrastic Dream 3   44

John's House   45

Directions   46

Swan Brothers 2   47

Red Fur Cello   48

Wonder   50

The Paradisial Vistas Available in *Uttermost Paradise Place*

For some years I've been attempting definitions of what is certainly an American surrealism. It descends from our luminaries of the absurd, Charles Simic and James Tate, and to a less direct but nonetheless evident extent, in the troubadour journeys of John Ashbery. This surrealism arises in part out of an idea of the American sublime that the films of Charlie Chaplin perfected. It depends upon a heart made pure by its impurity, and a predilection for accident derived from chance. In *Modern Times,* the tramp is released early from jail because of his good citizenship and, taking the first turn as a free man, a flag falls from above a construction into his open hand and he is suddenly leading a workers' march. Everything that the picaresque hero achieves is by accident, and his exploits never give him power; in fact, his very powerlessness is his strength. How is this delight in the non-authoritative American? How can it be categorized as surreal? While Magritte might never have guessed his bowler hat would sell t-shirts, it stands to reason that American versions of old world aesthetics would have to depart from ancestry in their own history. There would have to be comedy, cinema, and self-deprecation. We would be juvenile, carnal; we would try unselfconsciousness; as Frank O'Hara proposed in "Personism: "everything is in the poems...," i.e. There is no outside!, i.e There is only outside! Don't come looking for me here! As for technique: "If you're going to buy a pair of pants you want them to be tight enough so everyone will want to go to bed with you. There's nothing metaphysical about it." Alternately, the ultra-serious, psychoanalytic, deeply moral and political charges of André Breton's manifesto couldn't live easily in such a young (immature?) country, nor could the Latin American, deeply embodied surrealism of a Neruda or Vallejo suffice. And since our form of oppression has often been a consequence of a mistaken belief in our own freedom and autonomy, a surrealism connected to the blood trail of Eastern European history couldn't be ours either, though it's this connection that is most evident in the work of the young American surrealists working today—among which Laura McKee must be counted. The geography of our imaginations has mapped paths of carnage and resurrection similar to those of our Eastern European counterparts such as Vaska Popa, Zbigniew Herbert, Czeslaw Milosz and, more recently, Tomaz Salamun; if the paths are less strewn with bodies, it is only because of the comparative brevity of American history. To brave a comparison: the estranged self in Eastern European literature begins in the mass grave of its history and moves in its surrealism toward individual understanding, while the estranged self in American surrealism begins at the point of self to move outward into the unfolding history that is our country. We are leaving ourselves behind. When our surrealism fails, as it must, it is when the ontological circuit charting self and other becomes imbedded in self-reference. When it succeeds, as it must, it is when the trajectory of self swerves, like our *echt* Chaplinesque tramp, into the crazy parade that frees us all—for the moment. To quote O'Hara again: "Nobody should experience anything they don't need to, and if they don't need poetry, bully for them, I like the movies too. And after all, only Whitman and Crane and Williams, of the American poets, are better than the movies." I'd add a dozen more now, and I'd place this book in the running.

That is to say, the poems in *Uttermost Paradise Place* achieve transparency. While many of them are perceived via a persona, it is ultimately the personae of perception itself that proscribes the pure pleasure of reading. Aware of what commodity culture made of European surrealism's dependence upon the image, our poetry has evolved. Increasingly, the best poetry of American surrealism—or really, the best poetry written from any aesthetic or modality—is committed not only to the eye, which has its phonic and undeniable connection to the "I," but to the ear and the ever changing music available to it (and for this we are indebted to W.C. Williams, Louis Zukofsky and Robert Creeley, at the very least). The poems in *Uttermost Paradise Place* sound a music of syllables, repetitions, recurrences and duration:

> I found a flight suit in the dryer this weekend.
> The zippers were hotter than hell when it first emerged
> as if it were the machine's inaugural attempt at creation.
> When it fit perfectly, I realized it was perfect.
> Suit, I salute you. You have changed my questions.
> From now on, "What will I wear? I will wear the suit."
> Never again, "What will I wear? Those pants.
> But what shirt?"
>
> ("THE SOLUTION")

Charting a humor of consequence—hell is perpetually in this book and it is the Greek hell, where re-birth occurs—Laura McKee creates a poetics of call and response, but not in the traditional sense, as in poet to reader, chorus leader to singers, etc. These poems call to each other, syllable by syllable, and they are so pleased with their circuitry of sound and sense that readers—if they just give themselves away to the pleasure of being exactly nowhere but in the unscripted place all authentic poetry provides—will experience the paradise the book proposes. Perception doesn't make the world, nor does imagination. Things are real, words operate in relation in poems and their shapes instruct: "When it fit perfectly, I realized it was perfect." Bill Clinton could have just as easily said "it depends upon what it it is…" Noun and verbs, the nominative and the predicate have been separated out of fear of the transience which exists in language. "Suit, I salute you. You have changed my questions." How sweetly rare it is to overhear a poet's homage to her poem! Who authors who? As if we could answer!

Claudia Keelan

UTTERMOST

PARADISE

PLACE

What a Bad Idea to Come Out This Far

Let's all go down to the shore and whisper our sorrows to the water.
Let's all hold hands at the start of the year and stumble out a ways.
The reflection will screw our eyes shut and the water,
if nothing else, will cool us off when hell is burning
holes in our pockets. Let's all go down and whisper our sorrows
to each other. Your ears are least interesting to me in full sun. I don't mind
if we go to hell. Of all the places I've ever been, hell is the tune that sticks
with me most. Let's all hold hands and hum the hell out of it.
Let's all go down to the shore and burn holes in our pockets.
Maybe hell will slip out quietly — enough said among us — a vague shape
change in the shape of the water sinking and changing into the west.

Glacier 1

To her, beautiful land was like motion. She purchased a small corner
in the northern corner of the state. Nearby, the canyon was. I don't know
if she ever went by. The weather flung out its sheets and every morning and
every evening sudden depressions, climbs, racks of stratocumulus.
One afternoon we found the lip of a bowl and sat in the half shades,
for thousands of years. Her hand signaled and the distant ranchers moved their cattle
from one side to the other. Because of the distance I'd like to return. Of course I will.

The Solution

I found a flight suit in the dryer this weekend.
The zippers were hotter than hell when it first emerged
as if it were the machine's inaugural attempt at creation.
When it fit perfectly, I realized it was perfect.
Suit, I salute you. You have changed my questions.
From now on, "What will I wear? I will wear the suit."
Never again, "What will I wear? Those pants.
But what shirt?"

Sun On One

The surfaces are wrong.
Friend, if I walk alone a long hemisphere—
                                    like gone
                                    long long gone.
Don't I circle nervously when nervous.
Like a common error.

Geometry and a Letter

1.

The silver bowl walked to work this morning.
Along the way, many were so captivated by the silver bowl,
they could not help but exclaim, "there goes the silver bowl."
You have a remarkable bowl.

2.

The hula hoop rolls down the street without origin
like the inscrutable word that appears occasionally in a dream,
printed on the page, recognizable and undecipherable. All those years wasted
on penmanship. What use the "W?"

3.

Dearest A., I write to you, B., from exile.
See another end to a burning day at the end of my hand
where the dirigible heads madly for the horizon.

Billboard 1

Now there would be more underpinning to shore up their idea
                              that they had left,
                                    samples in their pockets to evince
        a rumored river bed. And seeing them caused me to wonder
                              where should we be from?
does a silver cloud have a lining? who would be our brilliant mother?

In a fox stole.
In rhinestones.
Oh note taker.

Pregnant Headless Clown

People are rushing into the room. A new window idles on its side
of the Goldfinch Brothers Glass and Glazing truck across the street.
Manual labor, I think, what a way to come back.
Then I pause before a costume shop display and because of how the light
is falling, appear suddenly to myself in a clown suit. "Tell me something, clown."
"I notice," said the clown, "that you are pregnant." As the room fills with people,
I meaningfully recount a sequence of events to anyone who will listen.
"First a squirrel ran past. Then a rabbit appeared on the lawn.
Later, I ran over a snake." The clown nods.
"All animals," I say, and watch closely for her reaction.

Wet Feet

The Sound shore is friction. Decay is gravity moving
out of earshot, absent from above
        until it rises
        until high time
for you, General Sisyphus, to straighten your collar
your army, your marbles, up dwindling from the channel water in too many columns
to add up. Whose behavior do you understand? That full clamorous eye
        causes our hair to part badly on the left horizon,
        causes a different endless shape, inconsistently wet feet
while stones back across the uncalm skip evenly toward the moon

Many Beautiful Stories

Which vary not very much in different portions of the earth
        though how should be put down
as general examples still.

A low flame landside slid gently beside them,
        distinguishing around her
a call to rally against, to take the crown.
Slowly the throne moved
        through and the city was whispering.

                Day after day would become their design and from
        which shamefully divided the world.
                        Shallow banks of sand.
Shimmering signal mirrors. Forays protrude
into the sea.

                Then later she was called a refuge and sent forward.
A cautionary only. No founder. No lighthouse.
        A conspicuous position
                is made of lighting
            is has not happened
and this is a model
the thought of which finds itself nearly two thousand miles from the rainy district.

They emerged from the discussion uniquely turned out and slowly it turns them
out where once they slept, exquisite against the foliage.

Ekphrastic Dream 1

The figure should be arrayed for battle
and positioned in an aggressive stance:
arms wide, legs wide, mouth open.
A second head sits on his forehead
whose mouth is open as well.
Colors should have a metallic gleam
and be suggestive of fire. The sky,
serving as a backdrop, should appear
to be in pieces as if he has just broken through
or wrenched himself from it. In either case,
the possibility of return should seem remote.
This fact may or may not influence the creature's fury.

Death of a Blue Vase

for S.G.

Who spilled all this water?

I mean this is one type of authority structure.

    ♔

The little lead soldiers from a former time creep up to the window
in ranks and report: it was the blinding sun-
light, clouds too, racing past.

        Once the ladder was secured upright to the bed
        the truck sped north like a superfluous question
                            interrupts a magic trick.

Who hung the leaden sky so low to the ground or doesn't want to go
somewhere when nothing slows us down.
                        Merrily merrily merrily.

I mean there is time to get us in order.

    ♔

The way some people tie boxes to the roof of their cars and set out
is so reassuring. I'd like them to tell me what to bring. I'd like them to swing by

and pick me up on their way out of town. Outward. Terrible thought just now
doesn't circle back around. Tack that to the drawing board.

        The lumpy silhouette speeding down the freeway was more of a
        Mayan pile than Aztec (she said you could see it in the cities).

Now that's a set of gods. We'll need knives tonight, dear.
Back to the silver drawer. I knew it wasn't luck in there. Back outside,

the rain stopped and the wind picked up. Cumulus speeding
off to the next zone
and while the stars hem and haw, so far
none have left and light continues to decide across the distance.
As if in time to faint music a swimmer slowly crawls back into view.

I mean an obvious journey is another way to go.

The Last Wall is a Strange Cool Puzzle

Left by a mason years ago. Love of love.
Beloved forehead, so cool to the touch,
you're not even trying. Sherlock, hold the vial
thought up to the light, not the social shattering easy sound
next door and then laughter, not fingerprints or happiness, but love
of love, absence, inscrutable center of a stone, volute
convulsive start of a wave under an earth's worth weight
of water. A likeness like nothing I've ever seen before.
One day, you promise, we will get to the heart of it. Unthinkable,
unembraceable, nothing to delve or divine. My very paradise,
you say, as if it does not back itself into the heart of something smaller.

Strategy for the Decline

The cyclists, who have toiled slowly toward,
pose now in awkward proportions roadside
beside their delicate machines
as if Pygmalion had just backed through
the curtain of early October light
after one last authorial sweep
over the winded musculature. The narrator whispers
that we are beyond a start from a divine startling
kiss. It is for the tired catalyst foot now
to lunge through the wobble leashing it
to its bargain with speed and the race
toward the valley floor whose flocks dissolve
into widening signatures heavenward off the page.

Notes from Mr. Aday

The high wind overhead was a sheet of ice and the crows slid by
                     throughout the start like a glimpse of a divisor
beneath the brightness. The new year was already beginning to double
over. At first quietly, as we filed in, someone tripped on the threshold.
Then louder.
It was as if he had been running for miles, she said, when he rose up
                          to the surface and asked for more time.

Later, it will be even harder to describe what we took away from the experience.
Something fine is clearly needed for a shape like that morning. Dawn
and her sister nervously playing with our toys. And edges,
        dull ash-colored edges of fields, instructions, the ground
                    and that too will stretch for miles.

After his chest annealed, little crumpled maps were found in his pockets,
memories like directions back to places that had become paradise
over time after their time had faded from them.
And when her voice returned to them to read them out for the class,
they did sound complete —
        like lanterns hung from a tree to capture our imagination while she spoke
until our minds twitched with a feeling for his catastrophe that is hard to put back
                      on its hook
and leave alone because it did not belong to us
and leave alone with nothing to show for the experience
             like a perfectly hard object or a gift for comparison.

A Finite Piece of Furniture-Sized Light

In medieval times, neither of us would have been described, being no more than peasants nor boasting an unusual feature such as a scar in the shape of a symbol or only four fingers on one hand. For the record, then, we were unknown when I abandoned my post and followed you deep into the heart of the copy machine. Late afternoon clouds floated unopened above the snow. I cannot say our time together was perfect. To be honest, I never listen and recently, through treachery, you had thrown out your back and muscle relaxants had done nothing for the pain except bring on a chatty, almost casual, sadness as we split open the Xerox in parts around us: I'm telling you, I'm telling you, I'm telling you. Forever is broken. No one will remember how phenomenal its shambles will seem. Play of light. Roar of the crowd. Smell of oranges. And nothing to go on. I think we are golden, yes, I think we are golden.

Swan Brothers 1

My favorite brother was the one for whom the story
did not fully undo itself, leaving one wing stir
on nights when the calling winds pick up
and the past beats ghostly south across the moon.
What were you out of my sight, swan brother,
that is fear or sorrow in our father's eyes
when he rests a hand on your changed shoulder—
where the human pattern slips away and the story shows
how easily the miraculous garment comes off,
which we had made to celebrate your return.

Unweighted Nymphs in Still Waters

"Does anyone use them? I mean on ponds or lakes in rushes for Browns or Rainbows. What
patterns do you prefer?"

Yes, yes, above the lake, they unfurl. Luminous figures. Anglers,
their small boats arranged like motionless altars, moving the unnatural
lines in and out of history over-
                                    head. Fluorescent yellow. Orange. Because of time.
Because the wrist jerks back as if it were a creature with time in it
to burn. Is it like a pulse? Not our pulse.
Is it bitten? Almost. Over and over. Resting
for a moment against the surface. Arresting
                    for a moment where the line unfolds and does not lead back
exactly to the start as one might hope or describe
how the wait does not takes us forever to describe.

The Tally

For example, in comparison, I have in my pocket
a map that was clearly drawn by an idiot.
The path doubles back and forth with frequent side trips
to a small hamlet where a one idea farmhand
who I can't forget labors through his only line
in the script. Day after day we study the paper:
there — where the next set of shadows is crossing the field.

Glacier 2

with a line from I.B.

On a little bit of stranded glacier, in the thin light
of earth's full height, the view was in blue ranges
before us and it was hard to say who threw the first
snowball. Because I was there. This is an opportunity
that may never occur again. *Kaboom. La la la la.*

Letter to My Aunt

Sometimes, you get to the top of a ladder and discover you're at the
wrong building.

JOSEPH CAMPBELL

"Any more questions about the fall?" The fall knocked my head ajar and a soul crept in.
It spends its days napping on the hide-away, answering the phone "Acme
Night Owl Service" or alternately "Edifice Architects, may I help you?"
These days, the air in the morning is cooler.
A blue sky and weaker sun host whispered conferences on the balcony.
We should stay. We're entitled. We should organize for a sense of mystery.
We could do better than the north wind's dwindling scarf of migratory ducks.
The soul has your manner: a handful of wings, a grin in its voice,
a little bit happier than you were perhaps. Sleeps a lot.
A good day walks it down and back along the six blocks between the cathedral
and movie theater. There's the house that hatches plots. There's the house
with the plastic lawn. "Sometimes a smaller circle will occur inside a larger circle."
Like that time a boy waiting at the corner found a View-Master near the stop sign.
I can see it as if I were there — the strange shape flung from the car,
as blue as the sky, fourteen extra larger pictures.

Smaller

Like a tailcoat. Yet it was not a tailcoat.

CATHY HORYN

1.

Like a hole piecemeal toward the west. Flying absenteeism at dawn. The crows
    scatter, their action having taken off
in a place changing into light.

We had stayed the night to work it out.
Sotto voce. Chalked in lines. Stretched shoulder
to shoulder
between loss and a complete loss
for words. The fall from the waist. An outward demonstration
of so many voices overhead.

Full daylight. Someone make a point.

See the piecemeal end of it, she said. Over the water, now, the point is smaller.
See the containers pivoting back for more. If it is not a tailcoat, she said,
then what should I call it?

2.

I had a luxury soul; she only wanted to sleep.
I had a monitor soul and she knew
I only wanted to sleep.
Lay her down gently in the hold,
gently down, down, down. Then I shaded my eyes
from the world and let the ship go.

Anderson

We left them deep in their embrace at the edge of the lot
                                    and the dark was so dark
           in that man-made place their laughter flickered back to us
                     through the howling wind
                     like light from a distant star.

Because the gods are "capricious and forgetful,"
                            we must remind them of what we want.
           That night,
           the two of us embrace.

Then an old clerk took back our key. A sleeping brindle dog lay twitching
                          at her heels. She couldn't recall
                          when last we were here
and called us by the wrong names,
which was one way to continue
on that night and the freeway another
           whose staggered red line was like day-
break ahead to pass the time before us.

Paper Cut

1.

What are they cooking up, those cooks
sitting at a table on the corner in the blinding early morning sun.
I think they're telling tales, in conference under their tall hats,
legs keeping up a swing shift inside long checkered pants.
I think they have something up their sleeve.

2.

On warm nights, with the doors to the house open,
chorus strains from the dogs I have never seen in daylight
chase through the rooms until one by one they fade to sirens
dropping underground over the last hill before the down-
town hospitals. And because in fairy tales
there are frequently three tries, a faltering human voice
is sometimes heard behind the pitches and shrieks of the dogs,
moving closer to the present moment with a handful of leashes
as if to sort out the problem by yanking it backward off its feet.
I remember it now, the last words I heard before waking,
"you have spoken to these ideas very well already."

3.

Didn't I see you stand up in the dusk?
Didn't I see you running so beautifully across the field,
looking of half a mind in the half light to never come back?
Didn't I see you stumble out of your shape and walk forward,
as careful as people at a rehearsal, staring at the name
on your scrap of paper like something you've never seen before.

4.

Deep in the timberland, she wandered.
Like paging through. And passing through the shade that stood
with the stands in columns she was a change
in how the light could fall. Deep in the timberland,
the wind picked up what it found as is it went the way someone who wants
will handle everything in the shop and cannot make
and cannot make a decision. Then something was torn quickly from a book.
A blank page from under the wing of a startled bird. The first place it stops
is never where it stops. Finally, there is always a rush to the next place.
And making the space between flights a hinge time is someone
angling a mirror up from the ground to see it — when next it disappears — better.

5.

Does the woman long and is she folded?
Yes, she is unseemly, speaking about
speaking about nothing or how like the sun
to put someone in her silhouette
where she flattens and argues:

"To seem or fold, to seem and burn.
Without seeming to we fold until burning,
we seem to burn again. Folded,
when you unfold in general, specifically
your longing, I burn." Folded unfolds

a white paper mask on which she has written,
"The head of a terrible wolf puts it on."
We are not the same yet, says the wolf
and turns to move away.

6.

We found a porcelain head floating at the edge of the lily pads
just a few inches beneath the surface. Algae followed the hairline
cracks across her face and where the church-like sunlight shone through
the water it lent a human cast—her head thrown back
in laughter as if she had decided midway through to stop and make another.
And now this head lives in that sound forever, lighter without its body,
enough to do with just a neck that can turn where it wants
in the cool translucent world that was within our reach
for a moment, that moment, if we had had a stick.

Glacier 3

Day forty-three. My initial high hopes for the lottery begin to waiver.
Also, I notice the glacier moves farther up the hill. Anyway,
she'll come around soon. I know she will.
Despite recent misgivings, I'll stand by my idea
for a castle. A castle, not a palace, a castle.
Isn't a palace just a castle in town?
What else could she possibly want?

Unlike Paradise

with a line from J.K.

The painting's viewpoint was uncanny
and the chickens seemed to hustle from the frame,
preferring the museum to their cramped farmyard coop.
The wind was blowing hard. Elbows ablaze,
she vigorously polished the floor. Sunlight
on the smell of lemons deepened. The orchard alleys
led us away. Showers were predicted that afternoon.
Afterwards, I knelt among the stray shards
and gathered. The timer would open against the wall
when it was time. Our minds were perfectly made,
you know, but we will not solve any problems.
This is the best painting of chickens that I have ever seen.
At the end of the day, people rushed from the building.

Women, Weight, and Weightlessness

One has a face as stern as a visitation.
Expertly she handles cuts out of the case
and onto the scale, beautiful under the fluorescent
glare. The lucky few who still have eyes look at her
with respect from their repose in the plastic grass.

One has a face as vague as a lullaby when she roars by us
on the pass. Her truck has a sign: support women
hunters. Her truck has a sign: buy U.S.
honey. She would be merciful, I think to myself,
when she kneels down in the grass and after.

I saw a fox trotting across a field, one field down
from the flock. We were on the move. It was spring.
There was motion in the air — bits of us
catching the light on all sides. Nothing is fair,
I think to myself, and the floor creaks.
Now you know where I am.

Billboard 2

The sign is clear and fair
in which her face is not like her mind
until hypnosis or her harp
intervenes. Trucks move back and forth across
from the crack of dawn to the end of time.
Glacier Cement Co. is making the city a heavier crisis
when it will be and the crisis is like guessing how many
of us are in a large glass jar at a carnival stand.
We all want to win so badly. I can't remember when.

Horses and Monarchs

In a far away land, it is about time she understood
and the labor of becoming transparent when one is
simultaneously least and expecting surprised her.

Matching glass jars are aligned on the shelf, a little ecosystem
for each of us—one stick, an attachment, and light to scale

our volumes up the wall.
On the opposite wall
a picture of the old west hangs its customary sun and seated hero
astride near the horizon on a bridle path and the bridle path is glowing.

One day others just transform.

Settle down, she shouts, while we horse around
in her opinion in her beautiful room. It is almost time for everything
and we haven't changed yet. She is an extraordinary host
        even when simultaneously she descends to kneel
among us. Her eyes are orange and black.
Paying attention after all, wings blink slowly on the ceiling.

Do Not Confuse Opportunity with Certainty

All my hopes for you—beautiful box in a locked room,
beautiful lock just below the collar bone.
        Out wide again, the sea becomes us with less,
a fold in a towel folding
around an opened castle.

We should never have come; we must go forward.

Like a mother, or how the blue skin of the sea stretches less
of forever further these days, checking the corners, searching out
each cast out jar, a solution for each amnesiac.

The sky will be as blank as a scar.

This time as a thief. The taste of it or not is
simultaneously. Now I'm missing a few stories.

Swan's Trail Road

with a line from R.K.

We haven't had the wind that was predicted.
Nor have I done enough to change your mind.
Like a blind hand seeking a door in the wall
you say there is forever in the way
it is a pattern. Follow me out
into this field. I want to know
what finds my way across. In all directions
it is as if the earth undoes itself
the more I make for it.
Late through the late fall
light, distant fires, acres loosen.
And then begins again that we stay here.
Swan's Trail road like stillness
whose eternity comes back year after year.

Billboard 3

A hot air balloon rises over a page
of the Himalayas and the glacier falls away
beneath us like a narrow room floating
above a glass dome. On the down slide,
I think, disappearance might not be so bad.
As the next balloon rises up out of
a golden sigh is holding its breath. Lost,
lost, lost. What are these rivers
pouring down through the lowland
where no two life rings are alike.

Care and Feeding of the Faux Fur Coat

Take your coat out to a snow-covered field for a scream.
Make shapes of its animal with your breath in the frozen air.
Stand in a silent stand of pines. Bury your hands
in its pockets and imagine it as it once was. Wail, wail,
wail until you become half of its grief. Take it to the groomer, the pound,
your psychologist. Tell them it's keeping you up at night.
Work regularly with your coat on language skills.
Pin notes to its sleeves: I love you so much.
This is all a lie. It's not you; it's me.

Afterlife

1.

I was floating near the ceiling of a fireproof city,
confessing my origins to the office fish:
"To the rising generation of my name and to the generations
yet to follow, this record of an _____ but _____
ancestry is respectfully inscribed."

2.

Which led me to think again about the afterlife.
I worried it would be too much like high school:
ancient secretaries, an inscrutable abacus on its shelf
in the math room, the burning smell of bleach rising
off the tables, and always those glowing cheerleaders
at work in the periphery, ruining my night vision.

As the heavenly doors swing open, I imagine how the glances
swivel toward me momentarily and then away in a perfect figure
eight around which my dismissal turns through infinity.
Perhaps it will no longer matter and I move forward
through the crowd, leaving my dismay to follow behind
enormous and forgotten. At most a feeble tug from time to time
causes me to wonder why a fine thread is tied to my wrist.

Or perhaps, my dismissal will matter forever. In the hall. In the diorama
of a revolution created with string and foil. In the later coolness of the dark
playing field above which the stars, or some afterlife equivalent,
continue to set the pattern in motion because of a story
I can almost remember if it were not for the sudden blinding sweep
that arcs out of nowhere into view to complete yet another useless circle
and land on the blank soles of her pristine tennis shoes.

Glacier 4

Paradise is on the floor above us.
In the late afternoon quiet, we can hear the participants
moving furniture around. It must be circle time.
It sounds like no one is in charge. Chairs
gouging the floor. Collisions. Very little coordination
in general. Then the building falls silent.
Where was I, she said, oh yes, speaking about a hot topic
these days. Gingerly she unfolds the idea of spirituality
like a rare and complex flower in the air before her mouth.
We lean forward to listen closely over a new sound
as the daily line of earthless unweighted trucks rattles
up the hill before somewhere a great hole is started yet.

Neighborhoods at Dusk

Perhaps we are touring the neighborhoods at dusk
       for a glimpse of the happiness in other people's lives.
       Golden and even-sided.
           Angling like geometry through the trees, crossing the lawn
           if someone has left a door open.

There is handwriting about it for the sadness of having
lost it. Even when I myself am content, there is handwriting
about it like a physical craving for nothing I have lost.

Make a note: the form of it should be solid.
             And heaviness in the shoulders.
Its faint curving sound is a gull cry out-
side the darkened auditorium
            if I press my ear to the wall
because it always must belong to the other person,
whoever first steps back into the blinding daylight
after a long and heart breaking play.

Ekphrastic Dream 2

for H.B.

Two famous women arrive at the campground ahead of us and stake out a site near the shore where the island strikes the curve in the Sound like the arm of a swimmer. A light mist hums to itself as it hangs its shifting curtains, and nearby islands appear to disappear like hunched figures pacing behind a screen. I ask the women if they happen to have seen a missing parakeet. The signs are posted throughout the island. KEEP AN EYE OUT, in capital letters, in layers on public boards and sides of outbuildings. IF YOU SEE THIS BIRD, PLACE IT IN A BOX AND CALL THIS NUMBER IMMEDIATELY. Like a rumor of a solution to a puzzle, the shore is alive with birds, none of which are missing. The missing bird is blue with the striking black and white marks of a topographical map on its head and wings. According to the map, the head is a steeper climb. Because I admire these women so much, I ask them if they would consider moving. Typical, I think, they have chosen the best site. According to one dictionary, a pit is typical of hell. Carefully, I study the little black and white markings. According to the map, hell is a steeper climb.

In this painting, there would be a typewriter balanced on a log near a campfire. A brightly colored bird (out of place) flies from the trees bordering the shore. Sunlight falls strangely from the wrong direction. Two famous women are consulting a map although clearly they have no intention of going anywhere. The sound of hammering perhaps draws the eye to a woman in the distance who is nailing a sign to a telephone pole: IF I SAW A BEAUTIFUL CREATURE, WOULDN'T YOU WANT ME TO POINT IT OUT?

Lockets

In a vine field narrow valley near the sea
(I send you along), the hum of insects
and rotting vegetation are enough material for a Greek
chorus for years (forget me not). But I won't look
if it is frightening. Nor was our stop at the shore
before we turned inland comforting
though now we stand well higher than the crop.
Small honed birds dive in and out
of the remainder. Animals groan in the distance.
(I am off) and cannot fix my position.
You, at twilight with your idea,
still searching for the perfect one.

Weak Anthropic Principle

for AMB

I come across some broken glass in a room. I had forgotten. Reassembled, the pieces form a regular surface and from it I infer the back screen door to the universe room. Our little house on the shore. In spring, my father removes the glass (and the door swings open: across the lawn, past tiny scale trucks and shovels.) Until Fall, having forgotten, I run through the door with both hands out. I come across some broken glass. Reassembled, the pieces form a regular surface—sunlight on the floor from which I infer my place at the center, tangibly warm, back and forth, light on my heels, motion in the trees. I come across some broken glass I had forgotten. Reassembled, the regular surface infers I am imminent, heedless, at the door, my voice. Full summer, hands out, we run toward the shore, past our castles to the water, with the dogs on our heels, changes and errors and changes throwing it out again. I had forgotten. Finally a shape: the letter "c" for the bay, wind dangling its pilot over the water. Reassembled, I remember. Broken glass at the door. A square of sun light. Our little house back on the shore. Every spring, my father removes the glass.

43

Ekphrastic Dream 3

There would be no reason:

underpinnings	earth
uttermost	earth
place	green earth
paradise	earth
edges of	earth red
dissolve	red red
within which	red blue
from the ground up	blue blue

At the end of the exam, hairpins litter the floor.

John's House

I love John. John loves his house. Therefore, I love John
's house. At least, I love the nasturtiums growing wild up
through the walk, nodding like sycophants in the heavy air
ahead of a storm as we make our way home. Anyway,
I love John. His ratty bathrobe. His depression.
I love his problems, the warmth of his skin, the miserable look
in his eye when he answers the door as if opening any door
were so laden with consequences it should always be cause
to step back and consider. Infinity, John, I say, what a good idea.
I've brought you some flowers. It doesn't look good for us
outside today. Horrible and coherent. Better to stay inside
given how much I love you, John. Though I do not love your house.

Directions

for D.L.

As you approach the entrance begin looking.
Pull over. Pull over and get out of the car.
Under the front will be a packet with a key
for the gate. Continue to the sign.
Turn right and continue.
The house is straight ahead and you enter.
Others coming after you will dial
and the house phone rings.
Answer it. When your visit is over, please leave.

Swan Brothers 2

We have found a little house on a tidal river.
At night, we can see the fires of the hobo
who has set up camp on the banks north of here.
I want to go to him for news of my father.
My swan brothers don't seem curious
at all. Only I have stolen out nights to the edge
of his camp and waited there until my resolve
fails. In the earliest hours of the morning,
the great heron (who has never spoken to me)
glides like a verdict pen up and down the river
crossing out word after word.

Red Fur Cello

1.

Whose heights are highly referential
our highly referential
view from here that keeps you upon
hearing an uproar at the palace
over the heist of you immediately
we left the saddest, saddest note
and badly spelled
to boot. They cried
upswept and searched
and searched
for days were not recovered
in.

2.

When I saw the woman pass by
in the guise of a giraffe,
I lamented—oh why had I not
considered choosing a mammal myself?
Overhead, the city's great crane arms
paused for the evening
to point out and concur. Her rolling,
infinite gait made less of us
with Brownian qualities not at
our speed—it made us for what we are,
that fits together, that stops.

3.

Not all music, but part of the mind.
Slower than a gull.
Slower than a helicopter clocked at sunset
between two buildings over
one block.
And then down.

4.

Unhindered, then, for a moment
we spent our time like a fall of golden coins—
wine and air and light at the end
at the end of the garden—
hemming and hawing over humming-
birds, or charming diagrams of them
and whether or not they make a sound.
They are quite violent,
these natives of the apple tree,
sometimes pictured as the lemon tree
across from the bar and parking lot
when I run out of red.

Wonder

for W.M.

The fox is at the back of the trailer, washing dishes in the dark;
headlights catch the plates as the cars sweep down the road.
Out of boredom, he'll occasionally accelerate the lunar cycle,
and lift a dripping full plate over his head, confusing motorists
who wonder where the time has gone. Later, he switches
between coverage of the Iditarod and the towing of Troll Station
out into the North Sea. The blue light flicker at the back
of the trailer is fraught with occasions for failure. In places,
the immense, cathedral-like structure barely clears the sea floor.
Should a storm arise, the station would tear itself apart.
But when the dog team takes a corner too fast and the lead dog is flung
against a tree, the speed at which the cursing driver leaps
off the sled to cut the animal from its traces
brings tears to his eyes. Now the driver runs
down a snowy, glowing path with the animal in his arms
and the slipping camera men follow to a barely lit exigency village
where the dog is handed through a door. The camera cuts
to an aerial shot of the North Sea, dwarfing Troll Station
inside a wide, unswerving opinion. The fox laughs
nervously, begins to sing, laughs nervously, sings a little.